Education Centered
Community Focused
Project Driven

a nonprofit education collaborative

A Trace Taylor and PCS Partnership Anthology
BIRDS by Pinellas County Elementary Teachers
A Trace Taylor Workshop during which teachers explore science,
language arts, and the instruction and application of writing.

Authors: Julie Poth, Mary Osborne, Annette Morrison, Barbara Khoury, Caprice Johnson, Christine Steiner, Dawn Avolt, Delonda Boyd, Ginande Jester, Judith Genewick, Keesha Graham, Kelly Czarnecki, Kimberly Dennison, Kristi Shultz, Laura Bemis, Mandy Glaser, Marge Siemon, Rachel McClure

Developmental Editor: Trace Taylor
Birds Curriculum Writers: Trace Taylor and Mary Osborne
Instructor-demonstrators: Trace Taylor, Mary Osborne, and Julie Poth
Project Manager: Mary Osborne
Managing Editor: Trace Taylor
Production Assistant: Susan Gilbert
Design and Layout: Tysha Lewis
Technical Proofreader: Athena Buell

Images: Shutterstock.com; http://www.webdesignhot.com/; https://www.free-clip-art.com; Ryan Lerch: Anhinga, p.27

ISBN 13: 978-1976107276
ISBN 10: 197610727X

First Edition, September 2017

Education Centered
Community Focused
Project Driven

a nonprofit education collaborative

Innovative, Project-Driven

Workshops

Focused Thematic Writing Experience Tailored to Fit Your Curriculum

Sentence Construction
Paragraph Construction
Essay Construction
Self-Editing
Point of View
Syntax
Vocabulary
Voice and Tone
Punctuation
Grammar
Tense
Research and Citing
Character Development
Scene Development
Active vs. Passive
Emergent Writing
Position Paper
Personal Narrative
Research Paper
Book Writing

Full Publishing Services to Meet All Project Needs

Professional Instruction
Mentorship/Coaching
Developmental Editing
Proofreading
Layout and Design
Illustration
ePub Creation
Photography
Digitizing
Project Management
Copyright Filing
Rights Management

Workshops result in published thematic compilations of participants' works.

Trace Taylor

ARC PRESS
Books

AMERICAN
READING COMPANY

AMERICAN • READING • COMPANY
COMMON CORE STANDARDS

Sponsor an Author or Workshop

MetLife
Foundation

CLL Press

CLL Writers Guides

Teacher PD Anthologies

Classroom Anthologies

Individual Student Works

CLL Curricula

- Built to Order on Topic of Choice
- Integrates Science & Language Arts
- Adaptive & Smartboard Friendly
- UDL Differential
- Standards Aligned
- Project Based

The Cross Creek Chronicle is a literary journal sponsored by Pinellas County for Pinellas students. Cross Creek's Managing Editor, Mary Osborne, serves as a Language Arts Staff Developer for Pinellas County Schools and as a Board Member of Community Leveraged Learning. Mary believes writing is key to the deeper understandings of subject matter and necessary for academic success.

Special Thanks to:

Julie Poth

Mary Osborne

Lisa Yacso

Paula Bellin

Athena Buelle

The Teachers of Pinellas County Schools

Pinellas County Parents

Trace Taylor

Table of Contents

Ginande Jester - 30

Keesha Graham - 34

Annette Morrison - 38

Delonda Boyd - 42

Caprice Johnson - 44

Christine Steiner - 46

Dawn Avolt - 50

Kristi Shultz - 52

Marge Siemon - 56

Julie Poth
Dept. Pinellas County Schools
Elementary Science

"My passion is helping teachers and children to be curious seekers of the world around them through Citizen Scientist Ornithology opportunities. My favorite quote that relates to this is, "If the bird and the book disagree, believe the bird."

Foreword:

Transformation

Imagine a teacher on the first day of summer vacation. Visualize what the day might be like. Maybe asleep, hidden under the covers from the morning sunshine that pierces the window. What about the aroma and taste of fresh coffee, the back and forth movement of a swing on the porch as words from a novel form and come to life in the mind? When I think of a teacher's first day of vacation, this is the image I conjure.

Twenty-four Pinellas County 4th and 5th-grade teachers painted a different picture of this day because they intentionally chose to attend the Community Leveraged Learning (CLL) Birds Workshop held on the Eckerd College Campus. Sometimes, the unexpected frames decisions that are made. It was the word bird in the title of this workshop that prompted me to forgo morning coffee on the porch to attend. Birds are my heart. However, as the day came to a close, it became evident that the guidance of Trace Taylor in the art of writing was the true reward.

The Birding Workshop, a multidisciplinary curriculum of science and language arts, edited by Mary Osborne, Literacy Staff Developer in Pinellas County schools, and written by Trace Taylor, founding CEO of CLL, provided an opportunity for teachers to learn about the science and history of birds while strengthening their instructional craft in writing fundamentals, which in turn will transfer to their students.

My introduction to Trace Taylor was a confirmation that committed people can do great things. She captured the attention of each teacher through sharing her low sweet laugh, gentle reflective thinking, and intense heart for science, words, and writing. Her effective facilitation guided each teacher through an intentional structure of innovative instruction, observation, activity, application, discussion, and revision. Each participant strengthened their craft while they created their topic relevant story.

BIRDS

by
4th and 5th Grade Pinellas County Teachers

Mary Osborne
ELA Instructional Staff Developer
Pinellas County Schools

"For more than thirty-five years the teaching of writing has been more than my daily work; it has been my life's passion. My goal has always been to help teachers and students learn what it means to be not just a good writer or a better writer, but most importantly, what it means to be a deliberate writer. They cannot be deliberate without being taught the writing tools needed to accomplish that objective. This workshop accomplished that and so more in a single Saturday. It is one of the most effective and enjoyable trainings I've ever attended."

For These Birds

Alfred Hitchcock's movie The Birds terrorizes me. I have watched it many times since it first appeared on March 28, 1963. In it, Melanie Daniels meets Mitch Brenner in a San Francisco pet store. He intrigues her, so she follows him home. She brings two lovebirds along and gives them to Mitch as a gift. He gets the hint. A romance commences before the terror begins.

It's a routine day when something gruesome happens. At Mitch's sister's birthday party, those lovebirds attack the children. The scene begins outdoors. Children gather to play a typical party game: blind man's bluff. In this game, a child's eyes are covered with a blindfold. The significance of eyes being protected is not lost when a flock of seagulls appears. At first it's just a few, and then it's a few more, and then more, until gulls outnumber humans. Attacking and pecking. No body part is safe, especially not the eyes.

In another scene, Melanie is trapped in a phone booth after escaping from an explosion at a gas station. Fire and birds threaten the townspeople, and Melanie is helpless to save them. The movie intensifies as more birds appear in each masterful scene. Although the locations change, the outcomes of each of those scenes remain the same. The sheer volume of birds is a big part of what makes the movie so terrifying. Trust me, it doesn't end well.

Today, I had a different experience related to birds. With binoculars around my neck, I joined some fellow teachers on a stroll to spot birds on the

Eckerd College campus. The campus itself sends out a secure radiance; it elicits a sense of peace and tranquility. But it is that first glimpse of a bird that transformed me. We no sooner walked a few feet from the classroom than we spotted a blue jay in the tree above us. He fluttered his wings and flitted from tree limb to tree limb. One by one, other jays joined him. I didn't worry that they squawked to plot my demise like those gulls and crows in Hitchcock's movie. Before long, the jay and his friends hopped, and screeched, and disappeared.

Soon we stopped to study a small bird with its long neck sticking out of the water. None of us could figure out what it was. Someone used their phone and within a moment identified it as an anhinga. This bird is sometimes known as the water-turkey. Their broad tails assist them in their favorite activity, swimming. Known also as the snake-bird, it is common for them to swim with just their long necks and heads sticking out of the water.

We walk a little more and then we see it: a gathering of twigs and leaves. Thick tree branches tucked among bits of moss create this home for birds. A nest. A safe place for a feathered family to thrive. Could it be? Seagulls huddled, warm and loving, together in peaceful tranquility. No threat, no fear. A new version of Hitchcock's gulls.

This day's adventure ended differently than Hitchcock's The Birds. By the end of this day, I had become a bird watcher, not out of fear, but instead out of awe and appreciation for these birds.

Bobbie Khoury
Mildred Helms Elementary
Curriculum Specialist

"Math and Science are my thing. My goal is to help teachers see how integrating these subjects into our transdisciplinary way of teaching will enable our students to express their curiosity about the world around them and their place in that world."

How to Become a Birdwatcher

A professional development workshop titled "Project-Based Writing and Publishing" sounded intriguing. A friend and colleague suggested we go, so we signed up. Upon arrival, we learned about birds. The PowerPoint presentation, the embedded videos, and the presenter piqued our curiosity about how we might possibly become bird watchers in one afternoon. The presenter, Trace Taylor, separated us into small groups and instructed us to "watch birds" from 10:45 – 11:30.

What are we supposed to do? I only knew the basics about birds: the red-headed ones that bang on things are woodpeckers; the blue ones are probably blue jays; most probably, the red-chested ones are robins. Let's see if we can put what we learned earlier that morning to good use. Our journey began. We walked and kept our eyes and ears open for movement and sounds, equipped with our pocket guide on local birds.

First stop was a pond with trees that skirt the perimeter. Eight white birds sat and preened themselves. Out came the guides. Which picture fits what we are seeing? Ah, the snowy egret matched perfectly. We used the process of elimination, wings, beak, size. No yellow, so they couldn't be cattle egret. Across the pond, an equal number of the snowy egrets hunted prey.

We realized this task was not only doable, but an enjoyable adventure. We continued to walk, observe, listen, and note. Each time we encountered a bird, we followed the same process: observe the bird and refer to the pocket guide. The reward came

when we observed a woodpecker banging on a palm
tree, two blue jays teasing each other, a bird on
a power wire too distant to identify, two osprey
involved in a loud conversation about something,
an anhinga with its wings spread majestically,
and a blue heron standing with one leg in the
pond where we began.

    The day was an exceptional way to immerse
oneself in the sights and sounds around us and
attach those sights and sounds to specific birds.
We felt like genuine citizen scientists! In the week
since this learning opportunity, I have taken note
of my surroundings daily. I have paid special
attention to what is flying around me and what
is perched in the trees. I am, perhaps, a bird watcher
for life.

Kelly Czarnecki
Sexton Elementary School
5th Grade

"I love teaching all subjects but my area of expertise would be Language Arts. Teaching for me is joy because I see the growth each student makes throughout the year (academically and socially), and I grow with them. This workshop provided me the tools, strategies, and experience through personal involvement needed to help my young writers become future authors."

The Royal Albatross

It's been 751 days since you left. My heart raced with fear, lost in this world. Thoughts flooded my mind and insomnia began. When my eyes closed again, I return to where I felt at peace. In this place, I feel safe.

****

The woman in white summons me. She's ethereal, gentle, and I trust her. She wears a long, layered white dress that flows in the robust wind. I do not question where this sudden gust comes from. In a world full of noise, the urge to ask where I am is strong. However, I choose not to. Instead, I study the woman. She grows taller and more intimidating, yet radiant in her glory. She reaches for a pair of black lace gloves and slides them on. These gloves are in contrast to the vivid white space that surrounds this place. Her arms, though so delicate, lift with ease and smooth motion. Up and down and up and down. I start to mimic her actions with envy. She smiles at me and our eyes lock. Her arms pick up speed with intent and determination. Her fingers spread wide and her arms elongate. At this point in my reverie, I realized the woman in white is not a woman at all.

A huge white bird is about to take flight right in front of me. Its feathered wingtips whir against the wind. The loud swoosh with each rise and fall of its enormous wings, spanning 11 feet, is enough to overwhelm me. The flight is effortless, my life in this moment transcendent.

This magnificent bird is the Royal

Albatross. With its regal, white-feathered body, light gray hooked bill, and webbed feet, the sleek black wingtips are unmistakable. These birds live up to 70 years and spend most of their life in flight over vast oceans. Their great wingspan takes full advantage of the wind to travel long distances without much effort. Some can even travel up to 10,000 miles in one trip without flapping their wings. They use a technique called dynamic soaring.

An albatross chooses a mate with patience and meticulous consideration; they mate for life and courtship can last as long as 50 years. They shower each other with love during their time together. Often they court in dance or touch with their beaks or necks. The partnership between a male and female Albatross is one of equal responsibilities where the female expresses voice and choice. The male does the labor for the nest, but if the female doesn't approve, the male rebuilds. Their dedication to one another knows no bounds. They live their lives in peace, love and harmony.

****

I wake up from a dream where everything was divine. I feel the warmth of my skin in my bed. The darkness fades and light seeps in; it bathes me with a renewed sense of self. It's been 751 days since you left, but now on Day 1, I'm free. In this, I feel confident.

Kim Dennison
IB-PYP Magnet Coordinator
Mildred Helms Elementary
International Studies Center

"I have been teaching and coaching students and teachers for almost 18 years. I love when my students, children and adults, have the AHA moment and their faces light up with knowledge and connection. This workshop reminded me about the power of real world writing. Observing and then writing about the natural world can take several avenues: informational writing, narrative writing, opinion writing, and hybrid writing."

Proposal

A pair.
She, statue-still in scrub pine tree.
He, statue-still in moss-covered oak.
She shows off her brown, mottled shoulder.
He cocks his head and launches,
Circles the lake, wings spread wide.
The shallow, murky water conceals his catch,
Shimmer. Ripple. Unaware offering.
Clawed foot flexes.
Launch.
Descend.
Loop.
Ascend.
SNAP!
Ascend!

The crooked, craggy oak beckons him.
The squirm and twist of his offering
Does not deter him.
He cries from the top of the craggy, crooked oak—
Screech. Scream. Screech.
Launch.
Descend.
Loop.
Ascend.
An aerial dance for one pair of eyes.
He lands at the nest.
And offers his catch.
A pair.

Laura Bemis
Northwest Elementary
4th Grade

"For me, teaching is a passion. Passion for learning, passion for growing, and passion for progress. This training restored my passion for viewing the world through a child's lens and taught me how to share my findings in a meaningful way. Trace Taylor knows how to deliver the best training ever!"

The Prize

Among the trees, wetlands, and grasslands, countless species reside, but if I slow down and observe their unique behaviors, I might be surprised by what I see: the romantic mourning doves above, afternoon kisses for life mates. Below them, white ibis wade in the pond, hopeful for an insect or two. Gulls giggle in the distance. They plot with diligence their all-too-conspicuous moves to plunder an afternoon snack from children at play. I must look closer to spy what only the careful, patient eye might spot: a majestic osprey in the distance, perched high. She patiently circles the lake while prey swims below the surface unaware. Anticipation of the perfect moment makes her talons quiver. Calculated. Cautious. Confident. Bystanders, we watch. Does she notice our watchful eye? Can she sense our awe? Blink and she'll be gone.
Swoop! Her wings flawlessly carry her back to the perch. In her claws, the prize!

Mandy E. Glaser
Sandy Lane Elementary
1st Grade

"I love ALL "chapters" of teaching, but am especially fond of reading and writing. My true joy of being a teacher is being able to share my love of learning with students and help create a positive mindset when it comes to education. This workshop is one of the most interesting and FUN workshops that I've ever attended. From start to finish, it was engaging and inspiring!"

Move, fly, forage.

Time to head out and observe birds on this steamy morning. The sun shines after days of typical Florida downpour, which also means unbashful bugs appear who like to bite and swarm around my bare ankles. Notebook and bird guide in hand with binoculars around my neck, I head out to the damp grounds. Swarmed together on a tree branch sit six white ibis and one hefty great white egret. The egret stands at the end of the crowded branch, tall and proud, prepared for the hunt.

Move, fly, forage.

The agile anhinga caught my eye while I wandered around with binoculars attached to my face. A treasured meal hung from the bird's mouth after a successful hunt. The length of his neck stretched up and down like a turtle's head in and out of his shell. The anhinga devoured his meal before a pesky onlooker could steal a bite.

Move, fly, forage.

At the next aquatic location, I discover two distracted ducks hidden on the water's edge who use a few stolen moments of peace to groom and fluff feathers. Meanwhile, an iconic osprey circles above in search of a fleshy midday snack. Bored from an unsuccessful hunt, he opts for a quiet moment on a perch high above. With his chest puffed out and his wings spread wide, the proud osprey showed off his dapper down and rested his weary claws.

Move, fly, forage.

A glimmer of white shines down from miles above. In slow motion, a flock of white ibis cut across a clear blue sky towards their next destination. A burst of chirps and screeches fill the tree canopy, their source hidden from probing bird-watcher eyes.

Rachel McClure
3rd Grade Science
Instructional Staff Developer

"My area of expertise is using instructional strategies and best practices to help teachers and students learn to the best of their ability. My joy of teaching is watching a student or teacher grow and change to be a successful learner. I love to watch the light bulb come on! From the workshop, I took away a new way of blending factual information in a narrative form to make facts more exciting, engaging, and interesting to read. I cannot wait to try this strategy with students when writing their unit final reflection in science!"

Birding at Eckerd College

Our trio of bird watchers trudge through the crunchy, dark grass. Along the way, we scan for birds with binoculars. Still heard but not seen by our eyes, tiny birds flit from branch to branch. They sing songs of different tones and volumes. I envy those who hear and recognize birds through their songs. Birding guides and binoculars and video camera and notebook in hand, we travel in packs. My hand-me-down digital camera in tow, I try to capture the birds in flight. My photography teacher's voice echoes in my mind. Blurry objects fill my lens. The birds fly too fast and too far away to capture their characteristics up close in snapshots. Afraid up close I'll scare the birds off, I creep farther away than my lens allows.

Stringy green and tan reeds litter the murky pond. Beams of sunlight leave puddles of vanilla on a pool of chocolate water. A muscovy duck ripples the surface. Her brilliant blue head and back contrast with pops of color on her face and beak. White ibis gather across the pond on lofty branches. They discuss the day's events through noises of joy. The enormous, leafy tree branches lean and quiver. One ibis launches himself to join his friends. The graceful ibis glides across the crowded pond with ease and strength. His friends stare as he lands. The group hovers on a weighted branch over the water and squawk greetings at one another. One lone cattle egret struts along the shore. Her head bobs up and down with the rhythm of her steps. Her feathers and shape resemble those of the ibis, but her slim body and lighter beak color set them apart. In the shallows of the tall reeds, a great egret hovers on one leg, head down to fluff a feather, too regal to acknowledge our presence.

Yellow tulips welcome our arrival. Their curved leaves spread against thick, straight stems. Modern, bright-colored buildings with lines carved into the side corner of the pond, contrast the dark, calm water. Ducks preen their feathers on the sandy shore. They pose to let us spot their glossy, blue stripe of shiny feathers. Water droplets slide off the mottled tails. A quick shake of their head throws water in all directions. Round, girthy curved necks contort to reach hind feathers. Beaks open for brief moments and close without sound.

To our right, smoky gray Spanish moss dangles off of low branches. It sways in a light and airy dance with the breeze. The trees show their age with outstretched gnarled limps. A multitude of birds perch and stand beyond the reach of my lens. An osprey flies overhead and swoops toward us. Its wings touch the sky in a v-shaped line. She lands in the tops of the tree. Her bold features emerge. Her white chest and belly protrude. A short, curved, sharp beak sticks out. The wide, black streak around her eyes catches my attention. The darker, back wings and feathers rest. The osprey contemplates our presence and glances at the pond in search for food. Perched near the sun, the glare casts her in shadow. She nods and bows in our direction. She slopes her head to get a better view. Curious about our purpose, she stares, head cocked to the side.

We search in all directions for more birds. My focus stops near the shoreline water birds who prance along the water's edge. A blue heron stands on one leg submerged in the water, the other leg bent underneath his body. His beak stretches towards us, a hint of a darker color on the tip. On the right, a tricolored heron's lanky, spotted neck mimics that of a giraffe. Unusual patterns cover his neck with alternate squares and circles of white and blue. Both herons acknowledge each other's presence. A competition for food begins while they walk in opposite directions.

Movement catches my eyes from where we stand. Branches bounce up and down with the weight of an anhinga. Like a fan, her feathers spread outward into the sun's rays. She calls us to take note of her. She keeps her wings extended. She maneuvers them. Quick flaps stroke the air and cool the turtles who sun on a log nearby. Not disturbed by her cool flaps, they bathe in a tidy row from largest to smallest in perfect tranquility. For the first time, I notice the increased temperature. Sweat tracks slowly down my back.

We continue through the overgrown blades of grass to travel to their position. An unexpected friend disturbs our path. A shriek halts my feet. No one moves. A pack member declares, "Snake! Snake!" She lifts her foot and hops backward with careful steps. Below her foot, weaved around the blades of grass, lay a small, juvenile banded water snake. Black bands evenly space themselves around its small, red, limp body. At the time, we didn't know that this snake was nonvenomous and only bites frogs, baby turtles, tadpoles, fish, and insects. The pattern of its scales and deep red color create a stark outline from the tall, dark green grass. Expecting the snake to move, we stood paralyzed. No movement. Curious and filled with notions that it may be "playing dead," the Go Pro camera pokes the snake in short jabs. No movement. Determined the snake is deceased, we discuss how the little snake might make a nice meal for one of the birds. No one offers to move the snake to a more visible location.

Grateful no one harmed any wildlife, we press on. A fish leaps into the air to gulp an unsuspecting bug. The plop of reentry is familiar. Ripples form small concentric circles. Another bird eyes the fish while perched on a nearby branch. The long, skinny beak lunges forward with alertness. Long, dark brown tail feathers cascade past his feet. Lighter feathers slide past his neck as he inches toward the ripples and waits. Patient for the second launch of the fish, another plop is heard. Ripples form again, but the fish is too quick for the bird. No lunch for the patient bird.

Across the sky, seagulls flock together in a whirlwind of shapes. White swerving dots arrange and rearrange themselves. Puffy, fluffy clouds play hide and seek with the flock. Some seagulls disappear and reappear in flashes of white streaks. As the seagulls move closer, their wings dart through the aqua sky. Out of reach to observe the details of their curves, I cannot tell their features. Never close enough to determine their kind, their cries echo towards us.

We stroll down the side of the street for fear of snakes in the grass. We encounter other wildlife. Squirrels scatter up and down the trees. Butterflies flutter across the open space. Insects and bugs skitter. The next pond is empty of birds. This pond is quiet, undisturbed, and still. We do not observe birds here because there are no tall trees for floaters, waders, dabblers, fishers, or diving birds. We walk past the quiet pond to reach the sidewalk lined with trees. One osprey perches on a tree. Another osprey lands on a gigantic cross on top of the circular building. We enjoy the shade of the trees and cut through the courtyard. The intensity of the heat returns when we leave the sheltered area. Time to exit the sun's intensity and return to the air conditioned classroom. After we had resigned from bird watching, a blue jay treats us to an appearance in the hot tar street. The baby blue feathers, sharp dark beak, and tuft of feathers across his head contrast the collar necklace and white markings on his feathers. A black stripe accents her distinguished gray splashes. The blue jay is buried in the leaves of the tree. We struggle to detect her location. She remains a spot of blue in a sea of brown.

Class continues. We write about our experiences and create our rough drafts. We learn about the craft of writing. Tired but satisfied, I leave class and head to my car. The lot close to the first pond lets me soak in the view one more time. The ibis are now huddled by the shore. There are more of them. They have flown from the top branches and grouped themselves by the trees. Some move into the water together. Some strut along the shore, but they are still close. I move closer to take a picture. The ibis seem wary of me. Some pause. Some move away at a fast pace. Some stop and stare. Others view me with curiosity.

Most continue on their way, undisturbed. The muscovy duck from earlier is nowhere to be found. The great egret no longer poses in the reeds. The cattle egret still bobs and weaves and high steps. A red-bellied woodpecker spies me from the branches above my head. I hear his arrival first with a rapid peck, peck, peck. The sound awakens my senses. He poses proud and upright on the oak branch. The red splash of color contrasts the brown leaves. The black and white spots, feathers, and belly linger. The beak continues a steady motion up and down on the wood. The loud, constant sound of quick movements startles the other birds. They retreat away from the noise. The red-bellied woodpecker is above my car. He sends me home with a melody of woody strikes. He is my last snapshot.

Judith Genewick
Bay Point Elementary,
5th Grade

"I enjoy helping young people improve their writing skills by letting them be free thinkers. Once students start to believe in themselves and their writing, most seem to enjoy sharpening their skills and learning new writing techniques. I enjoyed the workshop as it provided time to be outside in the sunshine and back to nature."

Skyway Bridge Pelican

Skyway Bridge Pelican
Guardrail zip liner
wings outstretched and steady
coastal commuter.
Blue-collar worker
beat DDT
fights
fishing line
food thieves
eye abrasion with every nourishment nosedive
survivor
pterosaur in the seascape of present day.

Anhinga

Eyes bigger than stomach
my super-sized snack
fights the narrow, tubular trip
down
down
down
my long slender neck
Slinky-like
gulp
gulp
gulp
Yum.

Ryan Lerch: Anhinga

Fish

Today I met my executioner
yanked out of my
watery home and into the
strong bill of a feather-clad beast
down
down
down
This is no water park ride
filled with excitement and anticipation
wiggle
wiggle
wiggle
No possibility of escape.

Ginande D. Jester
Calvin Hunsinger
Grades 3-5 SBMH (School Based Mental Health)

"ESE is my area of expertise, specialized in reading. My joy derives from observing students demonstrate understanding of the author's purpose in writing. I took away that writing involves persistence and refinement. (No matter what your desired field of expertise may be)."

Guided Bird Observation Activity

The observation of birds consists of observation,
patience, and silence.
Watch. Silent.
Twirl, whirl, speed and guile, creatures soar
above our heads.
Birds of prey on wind.
Harmonious, subtle, melodic colors greet observers
with Electrified chatter.
Swift predators glide nearby,
Swift dead silence.
Blue jays' motion stilled on branch,
Sway, in time with leaf.
Trees clutched together, rest in grassy field.
A pair of black grackles paces between
strands of grass.
Brown bunny eats and watches. Studies us
While we birdwatchers study it.
How many species here at Eckerd?
How many at home?
Peacock, scrub jay, red cardinal, heron, egret.
Crackle.
Movement.
A quick shuffle. I shift from left to right.
Too soon.
The blue jay motionless, chirps at another perched
atop.
Is it safe?
I approached.
Closer.
Closer.
The jostled jay joists in the crook of the juniper tree.
Brown bunny scampers away, into underbrush,

Beyond the reach of old oaks and red shouldered
hawks.
What's left to observe?
Classmates approach.
Ears keen for sounds of life in the branches.
No more cries of the osprey,
A grackle's raspy honk.
Birds spring to life in the absence of death
overhead.
Two jays bicker with a crow.
Cardinals squabble over a perch.
Sparrows dance mid air.
Mallards flutter and preen.
Shadows mingle with undergrowth and cloud
cover.
Time to go back in.

Keesha Graham
Sexton Elementary, ELA Centers
3rd Grade

"Teaching has been my passion since I was 6 years old. It was ingrained in my head that I would never overcome my circumstances that life dealt me as a child. I love reaching children in ways that others thought was impossible. This workshop gave me the opportunity to reach my creativity at new levels and strengthen my writing."

THAT Osprey

Feathers fall from the sky. THAT famished osprey circles the pond beneath her. Over and over and over again. She refuses to rush; she knows what she wants. The delay bothers her not one bit.

Below, frantic fish carry on with their day in the underwater world around them. Their pathways look like a busy sidewalk on a crowded college campus. Each fish bumps into the next as they pass by. Where creatures without fins travel freely and magical light called fire burns, life above water seems like a myth.

In an oversized oak tree, two blue jays perch on a branch. They watch THAT osprey with their whimsical sense of humor. A great satisfaction builds up inside them for cleverly obtaining front row seats to watch the show presented in front of them. Their raucous chirps and laughs grow louder, but this does not faze THAT osprey. She concentrates on the pooled prize below. The fish look like glazed candy that sit, perfect, in a clear glass bowl. THAT osprey, calm and collected, wings spread wide, keeps her calm and glides on the breeze underneath her white belly. The sun's golden shine glistens all around her.

The fish below swim now in school. In school, they follow directions. One fish, no, THAT fish swims away. THAT fish appears different from the rest. Full of life, adventure, and wonder, he swims to the coast. He observes what surrounds him on the left and the right while the space above the water remains out of his sight.

THAT osprey focuses her eyes on the newfound prize. She circles the pond one final time. Her heart beats fast and at last, the time has come. In a nosedive position, she makes one swift move. SPLASH!

THAT fish is plucked like a lobster from a tank. Uprooted from his home. THAT osprey, now self-gratified, lets out a high-pitched call of pride. She wings back to her nest. She likes her dinner organic and raw.

THAT fish locked away in talons below, now knows what life above water looks like. THAT osprey arrives just as THAT fish takes his last breath. The blue jays on the oak tree fly away as the show comes to an end. Their conversation fades in the distance. School ends for the fish down below. THAT fish with adventure and wonder lives no more, but THAT osprey sits perched, full to the core.

Annette Morrison
Annette C. Morrison
Skycrest Elementary
3rd Grade

"My passion for literacy is shared with my students. My enthusiasm for teaching literacy in all content areas has increased their love of reading and writing! The purpose of attending the writing workshop was to help my students become better writers. I'd like to personally thank the facilitator, Trace Taylor for inspiring me to do just that!"

Bird Watch

Sarah woke to a repertoire of clucks, cackles and squawks. She peered out of her oversized bedroom window and blinked a few times at the typical sunny Gulfport morning. Her sleepy eyes followed the raucous of sound to a low lying branch of a century oak tree a few yards back to the edge of a miniature pond.

Not familiar with this particular bird species, Sarah reached for her nightstand and pulled out a bird guide and handy compact binoculars.

White head markings with vibrant apple-red beaks resembled a kind of tropical Floridian wetland flower. Sapphire and emerald wings glimmered and lifted violet-colored breasts and backs resembling softened brown clay. Shortened, slender, yellowish legs carried the birds in grand leaps from branch, to earth, and into the pond. With the support of their long toes, they walked atop the floating vegetation to gather strands of weeds and fill their beaks. One bird pecked with precision in a back and forth motion at the overgrowth of water thyme. Another jerked its head in a violent frenzy at the surface of the water. Sarah watched in complete fascination; she used the bird guide as a reference and discovered it must be the Common Gallinule that came to visit her on this otherwise normal day.

Sarah climbed out of bed in a hurried fashion and made her way downstairs. One scoop, two scoops, three scoops went into the coffee filter. Oh, how the smell of fresh coffee roused her senses in the morning. After the brew cycle ended, she poured herself a cup and walked over to the breakfast nook to recline in a chair. Sarah wondered what drew the birds with the red beaks and questioned to herself why she hadn't seen them before. While she sipped her morning pleasure, she peeked outside to watch her new friends delight in the overgrowth of vegetation. Just then, her thoughts were interrupted by the sound of the clock that hung above the kitchen pantry. The hour hand pointed to the seven and the minute hand on the twelve. "On no," gasped Sarah as she managed to gulp down her last few sips of coffee. Up the stairs and back down in record time, ready for the office and out the front door.

On her drive to work, she thought about the birds with the hope that her new friends would be permanent visitors, and if not, she found the company of red beaks, gem and brown-colored bodies, and funny looking legs to be quite pleasing and would welcome them back at their leisure.

Delonda Boyd
Pinellas Park Elementary
4th Grade

"As a native Floridian, I have always loved the natural beauty of our state, but this workshop gave me a new found appreciation for nature and specifically for the birds that inhabit it. Science instruction combined with the art of writing is a natural way to engage children and adults in fun, active meaningful learning. It also provides us with a deeper appreciation of the world around us."

The Woodpecker

As I walk along the well-manicured college campus, I pay attention to the wonders around me that often are forgotten in my day-to-day busy world. Squirrels screech and scuttle from ground to tree and tree to ground. A cluster of ibis jab the ground in search of food, an osprey perches high and regal in a lofty pine, blue jays dash in and out of shrubs, and seagulls squawk and hover high above it all. On this sundrenched day, the squirrels and birds scurry about. The woodpecker appears, the holy grail of bird watching in a common Florida sky of blue jays, seagulls, and doves. Along the tree, a bob of crimson crown and speckled zebra-backed body bounces up the tree trunk. The rose head darts from side to side as it ascends the palm. A lifeless tan frond crackles and falls at my feet. A faint blushed belly brushes against the trunk of the tree. A peck. Another peck. Peck! Peck! Peck! The woodpecker's pointy beak hammers the tree, a consistent beat. It probes and drills into the trunk. Does it pursue seeds, berries, or insects? Will it excavate a hole for a nest? I watch and ponder this behavior, but too soon, it departs, darts from tree to tree. I hear its churr, churr, churr sound fade.

Caprice Johnson
Pinellas Central Elementary, 4th Grade

OSPREY

Osprey, osprey where are you?
Do you soar, rest, or perch in a tree?
Where could you be?

I hear the gigantic osprey's call.
The sound fades away.
I yearn to see its long black wings.

I look up to the sky and see the sneaky predator
swoop towards the pond.
Seconds later, the osprey snags a slippery serpent.

I gasp and stare, awed by its glorious catch.
The osprey soars out of sight.

Osprey, osprey where are you?
Do you soar, rest or perch in a tree?
Where could you be?

Christine Steiner
Bauder Elementary, 5th Grade

The Trick to Bird Watching

Our group wandered the path in light conversation until we spotted a tricolored heron in the quiet pond. We stopped our chatter and snuck up close to marvel at its long and pointy blue beak, its steel-blue wings, and the soft rusty-pink feathers at the base of its neck. Silent, we watched it wait, statue-still, for small fish to swim by. It struck out and, in a blink, captured its meal in its sharp beak. We continued our walk, lost in thoughts of how it might feel to have to hunt for our food like that. Silence and stealth are tricks we'd have to practice.

We continued on with renewed interest. Dark-winged shapes darted in and out of the massive oak trees, too quick to be identified. Our pace slowed and we disappeared in dappled pine shade. I inspected the branches above our heads and spotted an inhabited nest hidden in the crook of a branch. Two fuzzy brown heads bobbed and weaved. Baby yellow-crowned night herons studied their unfamiliar world. A tiny motion drew my focus to a nearby limb. There, perched in the branches above the nest, was Mother, a silent sentinel over the safety of her young. Her yellow crown trembled, but her gaze returned to the sky once she concluded we represented little or not threat. We considered what it might be like, having to guard our young like that. Observance is a trick we'd have to practice.

Our group charged on, inspired. We rounded a bend. Dozens of crows met our intrusion with squawks of displeasure, so we headed off toward the dark, still water of another pond. We waited silent at the water's edge. A sleek, powerful osprey circled overhead in search of fish. Another sat near us on a low branch and sent up occasional warning calls. One of us moved too close. It took off in a burst of noise and feathers. We ambled on around the next bend and were rewarded with a familiar Tap, Tap, Tap. All heads pivoted in the direction of the sound and scoured the trees for its source. We caught sight of the brilliant red head and black and white body of a pileated woodpecker. It hammered away at a weathered tree trunk, and then just like that, flickered off in a blur of black and white. Our hearts skipped with joy over the fleeting glimpse. Clearly, two tricks we'd have to practice are patience and persistence.

A glance at the clock on my phone signaled the end of our birding activity, so we beelined for the air-conditioned classroom. In the cool comfort of the room, we discussed what we'd learned that morning: with silence, stealth, observation, patience, and persistence, we experienced a morning in the lives of the local birds.

Dawn Avolt
Pinellas Central Elementary, 4th Grade

A Walk with Birds

I walked across the springy lawn in the bright morning heat towards the small pond. Large oak trees congregated at the edges of a small lagoon. Sunlight bounced off the surface of the dark water while, across the pond, ducks swam near the tall weeds. From the branches of the young oak tree next to me, an osprey's call rent the air. My eyes searched the branches for the source of the fierce cry and found the powerful bird amongst the foliage; its watchful eyes sized me up. I crept closer to the oak in which it stood sentry. I had never been this close to an osprey before! I moved in for a better look, and a second call ripped through the air, warning me, no further. When I did not heed the admonition, the massive bird took flight, wings spread wide and gliding to the other side of the pond in search of refuge from the threat it perceived me to be. The raptor's sharp eyes caught sight of something in the water's depths, so it swooped low, claws stretched down towards the promise of prey. Talons broke the smooth surface of the water once, then twice. Unsuccessful, the mighty bird lifted empty talons and rose high with a cry of frustration. The large birded headed for the opposite shore and a rest on a branch that reached out over the small body of water. It gazed at me for a moment, sizing up the distance between us. Distanced from my intrusion, its sharp eyes resumed their scan of the water for the possibility of a meal.

Kristi Shultz
Perkins Elementary
5th Grade

Birding

Incandescent lights shine artificial white light. A soft buzz hums above our heads. Keys of computers tap at a vigorous pace. Pens scribe across pages while teachers take notes. Others inquire about FSA scores just released. Shushes and whispers about notes that may have been missed or clarifying information, "Did you get that?" "What did she say again?" "I never knew that?" "How did your students perform?" Artificially cool air chills the room, so frigid that I can forget it's Florida.

A teacher, now a student, leans back in soft-green cushioned seats with backs that recline just enough to make it bearable. Spoiled. We don't have these at my school. A rear wall is lined with aluminum trays loaded with decadent sugary donuts cradled next to non-dairy, gluten-free muffins. Colorful fruit sits while the teacher ponders the choice. What will it be today: healthy or unhealthy? Both beckon. Spoiled. Again.

Welcome to an infamous "sit-and-get" professional development. Welcome to work-through-your-summer. Welcome to Eckerd College, first non-rainy day of the second week of summer, which so many non-teachers refer to as a teacher's time-off. Please excuse the slight smell of a nearby waste treatment center and the overwhelming powdery smell of cleaner emanating from the women's restroom.

Welcome to Project-based Writing.

Tables of two, filled with crayons, scented Playdough (never knew they made such a thing), primary-colored origami paper, numerous bird references and origami instruction handouts, sticky notes, Sharpie highlighters, a copy of the CLL 2017 Human Rights anthology by Boca Ciega High School 9th-graders, and the CLL Writers Guide, 2nd Edition by Trace Taylor. My interest is sparked. Human Rights, Birds, Writing, Trace Taylor. Welcome to Project-based Writing.

Casual introductions are made, and so it begins. How does all of this fit together? What is Project-based Writing? Well, Project-based Writing, for today, is a 10 hour component that equates to 7 hours today and 3 hours of work to follow. Translation: training and learning does not end here. Project-based Writing is essentially a framework of writing instruction into which a thematic study is inserted. Today involves exploration, cameras, writing, and revising. It will continue with critiquing, analyzing, revising, and rewriting. Did I mention rewriting? Wait a second... one attempt is apparently not enough?

And so, it continues. Birds. What are they? Endothermic, vertebrate, dinosaurs classified by posture: whether they stand upright on two legs or on all four legs.

Foraging: what, where, and how. Lastly, flight: style, number of wingbeats, directness of flight; do they soar like an eagle or teeter like a turkey vulture? An excited, energetic, fluorescent-pink tee-shirt clad speaker attempts to compress her vast knowledge of anthropology, earth science, life science, and creative writing into an image-filled PowerPoint presentation meant to keep her focused on "birds." We will be writing about "birds." She continues and explains that these are natives of Florida. Displayed vocabulary forms a bird Wordle. Bird diagrams carefully labeled with new scientific vocabulary make me realize my lack of knowledge. A short, precise and science-based how-to bird identification video is delivered by kids for kids.

Lights are reignited. Artificial white-light drowns a dark, drab ecru room. This is only the beginning. An uncomfortable silence settles on us as a room full of teachers begin to question what comes next.

Freedom? Freedom to explore the Eckerd College Campus, freedom to search, freedom to observe, freedom to capture video, freedom to identify, freedom to find elusive birds that chirp, soar, hunt, and swim in this sunlit day. Opportunities abound.

Marge Siemon
Highland Lakes Elementary
4th Grade

For the Love of Bird Watching

My love of bird watching started very early in life. My family's big Friday night event always seemed to be to make a brown paper bag of popcorn and go to the Flagler Museum and watch Audubon Films. Back then, most families lacked color televisions. Very few shows aired on television, so the only way to see them was to go somewhere where the original movies were being shown. My parents made sure that all of us behaved while there and that we refrained from mischief. That never became an issue since what we saw fascinated all of us. These experiences exposed us all to the differences in the world and the beauty in all living things. Growing up in South Florida, we saw many kinds of birds and other animals, but we lived in town, and the population of wildlife was lower than you could imagine. At the Audubon shows, we learned about a whole world of birds, animals, and plants. My love of bird watching started there. To this day, I find myself, my eyes constantly watching the skies to see what might be out there. It is an awe-inspiring sight to see eagles, osprey, and kites soar in the air.

I share my love of bird watching in the classroom. Every year, one night a week, part of my students' homework is to go outside and watch birds. As every year begins, students tell me they see no birds at their house. When asked if they went outside to look, most say, "No." They just looked out the window. Our children spend too much time inside, and the whole other world outside remains unknown. From bird watches at school, they begin to recognize different birds that they have seen in their neighborhoods. The number of birds they see increases, and they become skilled bird watchers and report on a variety of birds.

I believe the adults in the lives of these students must show them the natural world in which they live and teach them to appreciate the beauty of it.

www.ingramcontent.com/pod-product-compliance
Lightning Source LLC
Chambersburg PA
CBHW071235240726